COMMUNICATION IN MARRIAGE

A Companion Workbook for Couples

MARCUS & ASHLEY KUSI

ISBN-13: 978-0-9987291-9-0

Join Our Email Community

To receive email updates about future books, courses, workshops and more, visit the website below to join our book fan community today.

www.ourpeacefulfamily.com/bookfan

Dedication

To all the couples out there doing their best to have a healthy and fulfilling marriage.

Table of Contents

Overview of This Companion Workbook

We are honored that you have chosen our workbook to enhance communication in your marriage.

In this complementary communication workbook, we will dive in and take a closer look at the communication lessons and skills from our book *Communication in Marriage: How to Communicate with Your Spouse Without Fighting, 2nd Edition.* More specifically, how you can implement the communication strategies you learned from this book in your marriage.

In *Communication in Marriage,* we shared examples from our own marriage struggles, showing you the practical ways we used different communication strategies to communicate effectively.

Now, with this complementary workbook, we want to help you devise a plan to avoid the mistakes we made. We will go through each chapter, step by step, and show how you can apply the communication strategies in your marriage.

So, grab a pen, your spouse and have a seat at our table.

How to Use This Complementary Workbook

First, read the book *Communication in Marriage: How to Communicate Without Fighting* alongside this complementary workbook. We encourage you to go through this workbook at your own pace with your spouse. There is a lot of information, so please don't feel like you must complete a whole chapter's worth in a day.

Second, to ensure you complete this workbook, schedule a consistent weekly or daily time to do the workbook with your spouse. At least 30 minutes a session will be required.

One simple way to accomplish this is to read a chapter of the book during the week and then complete the workbook for that chapter during the weekend.

Lastly, as you complete this workbook, try to keep an open mind, be patient, be honest with your thoughts, and listen to your spouse with empathy.

INTRODUCTION

Read the introduction on pages 1-6

Can either of you think of any aspect of your marriage that
does not involve communication?

_____

_____

_____

_____

_____

First, write down who will be identified as _You_ _____ and who will be
identified as _Me_ _____ throughout the remainder of this workbook.

Take the time to write down your top 3 goals as a couple for using this workbook:

1. _____

2. _____

3. _____

What do you think is your biggest struggle when it comes to communicating with your spouse?

You: _____

_____

_____

_____

_____

Me: _____

_____

_____

_____

_____

What do you think your spouse's biggest challenge is when it comes to communicating?

You: _____

_____

_____

_____

_____

Me: _____

_____

_____

_____

_____

Do you believe that you both have an equivalent say in decisions in your marriage and life? Do your opinions matter equally in everything? Why or why not?

You: _____

_____

_____

_____

_____

Me: _____

_____

_____

_____

_____

What are some topics that you have the most difficulty communicating effectively about as a couple?

You:

1. _____

2. _____

3. _____

Me:

1. _____

2. _____

3. _____

Circle where you think you fall on the one-to-ten scale of communication:

You: 1   2   3   4   5   6   7   8   9   10

Me: 1   2   3   4   5   6   7   8   9   10

Write down the main issue that you cannot seem to agree on or resolve:

_____

_____

_____

_____

Chapter 1

Read We All Communicate Differently, pages 7-14

What does effective communication mean to you?

You: _____

_____

_____

_____

_____

Me: _____

_____

_____

_____

_____

What kinds of conversations do you enjoy having with your spouse?

You: _____

_____

_____

_____

_____

Me: _____

_____

_____

_____

In this section of chapter one (pages 9-12), you learned about the four different communication styles that people use to send or receive messages the most effectively.

Circle which style(s) of communication that you use:

You:	Analytical	Intuitive	Functional	Personal
Me:	Analytical	Intuitive	Functional	Personal

How will knowing the style your spouse sends and receives messages help you when you are trying to communicate more effectively with them?

You: _____

_____

_____

_____

Me: _____

_____

_____

_____

After knowing what style of communication your spouse uses, how are you specifically going to change the way you try to communicate with them?

You: _____

_____

_____

_____

_____

Me: _____

_____

_____

_____

_____

Knowing your communication styles, how can you change your approach when you are trying to communicate about one of the topics that you have struggles conveying effectively that you previously listed in the introduction section?

Topic 1: _____

You: _____

_____

_____

_____

_____

Me: _____

_____

_____

_____

_____

Topic 2: _____

You: _____

_____

_____

_____

_____

Me: _____

_____

_____

_____

_____

Topic 3: _____

You: _____

_____

_____

_____

_____

Me: _____

_____

_____

_____

_____

Topic 4: _____

You: _____

_____

_____

_____

_____

Me: _____

_____

_____

_____

_____

Topic 5: _____

You: _____

_____

_____

_____

_____

Me: _____

_____

_____

_____

_____

Topic 6: _____

You: _____

_____

_____

_____

_____

Me: _____

_____

_____

_____

_____

How do your styles of communication complement each other?

_____

_____

_____

_____

_____

What are some tools, like the ones we mentioned (diagrams or taking breaks), that would be the most helpful when trying to communicate something to your spouse but have hit a wall?

_____

_____

_____

_____

_____

YOUR EXPECTATIONS AFFECT HOW YOU COMMUNICATE

Read Your Expectations Affect How You Communicate, pages 14-21

How was your family's culture growing up different than your spouse's?

You: _____

_____

_____

_____

_____

Me: _____

_____

_____

_____

_____

How were they similar?

You: _____

_____

_____

_____

_____

Me: _____

_____

_____

_____

_____

What were 5 of your expectations of marriage *before* you got married? What did you imagine your role and your spouse's role would be? What did you assume your marriage would be like?

You:

1. _____

_____

_____

_____

2. _____

_____

_____

_____

3. _____

_____

_____

_____

4. _____

_____

_____

_____

_____

5. _____

_____

_____

_____

_____

Me:

1. _____

_____

_____

_____

_____

2. _____

_____

_____

_____

_____

3. _____

_____

_____

_____

_____

4. _____

_____

_____

_____

_____

5. _____

_____

_____

_____

_____

» Discuss how your expectations were different from, or similar to, your spouse's pre-marriage expectations.

What are some of your expectations now?
What is your role and your spouse's role in your marriage?

You: _____

_____

_____

_____

_____

_____

_____

Me: _____

_____

_____

_____

_____

_____

_____

» Sometimes we have unsaid expectations and then wonder why we are always disappointed when our spouse fails to meet them. Take this time to start a conversation about any expectations you might not have talked to each other about and find out where each of you is willing to compromise. You may need more time than one sitting.

If you could have changed one thing about your family life growing up, what would it be?

You: _____

_____

_____

_____

_____

Me: _____

_____

_____

_____

If you could replicate one thing from your parents' marriage, what would it be?

You: _____

_____

_____

_____

_____

Me: _____

_____

_____

_____

_____

Can you think of any expectations you may have when it comes to communication with your spouse?

You: _____

_____

_____

_____

_____

Me: _____

_____

_____

_____

_____

» Communicate with each other, not only what communication expectations you have but why you have them. What do they mean to you? Why are these expectations so important to you?

» Can you think of miscommunications or disagreements you had that revolved around a single word?

Words can have different meanings to different people, depending on individual experiences and understanding. List 5 words or phrases your spouse uses that have a different meaning to you, and what your expectations are when you use them. Then, discuss where you think your expectations come from.

You:

1. _____

_____

2. _____

_____

3. _____

_____

4. _____

_____

5. _____

_____

Me:

1. _____

_____

2. _____

_____

3. _____

_____

4. _____

_____

5. _____

_____

Non-Verbal Communication

Read Non-Verbal Communication: Body Language, pages 22-24

Do you tell your spouse that you are "fine" even when that is not the case?

You:	Yes	No
Me:	Yes	No

Do you expect your spouse to read your body language and press further?

You:	Yes	No
Me:	Yes	No

» Think about a recent disagreement you had and how your body language was speaking to your spouse. Were your arms crossed? Did you roll your eyes or shake your head? Were you calm and showing them you were listening with an open mind?

What could you do better next time, while being conscious of your body language?

You: _____

_____

_____

_____

Me: _____

_____

_____

_____

_____

What body language do you prefer your spouse not use when communicating with you?

You: _____

_____

_____

_____

_____

Me: _____

_____

_____

_____

_____

Most Common Communication Mistakes in Marriage

Read Most Common Communication Mistakes in Marriage, pages 24-25

Circle which of these common communication mistakes you make when you try to communicate with your spouse.

Assuming. Instead of listening to understand what your spouse is saying, you are impatiently waiting for them to break for a second so you can say your bit. Or you don't wait and interrupt them.

You   Me

Selective listening. Multitasking can sometimes be the culprit. Are you distracted by your phone, the television, or the endless to-do list in your mind?

You   Me

Yelling. Raising your voice to be heard only puts the other person into defense mode and defeats the purpose.

You   Me

Defensiveness. Being on the defense means not being willing to try to see things from your spouse's point of view.

You   Me

Criticism. Being overly critical will erode any progress you have made in communicating with your spouse.

You   Me

Contempt. Displaying feelings of resentment and strong dislike for your spouse is a huge road block to communicating.

You   Me

Stonewalling. The silent treatment, shutting down or whatever you want to call it, will bring any communication attempt to a screeching halt.

You   Me

Pretending you understand. If you don't know what your spouse is talking about, then admit it. Pretending you understand is very misleading.

You   Me

Expectations. Preconceived beliefs, closed-mindedness, and expectations that are not verbalized can leave one or both of you very disappointed and not on the same page.

You   Me

After knowing which mistakes you are making when it comes to communicating with your spouse, how best can you avoid each mistake?

Assuming:

You: _____

_____

_____

_____

Me: _____

_____

_____

_____

Selective Listening:

You: _____

_____

_____

_____

Me: _____

_____

_____

_____

Yelling:

You: _____

_____

_____

_____

_____

Me: _____

_____

_____

_____

_____

Defensiveness:

You: _____

_____

_____

_____

_____

Me: _____

_____

_____

_____

_____

Criticism:

You: _____

_____

_____

_____

_____

Me: _____

_____

_____

_____

_____

Contempt:

You: _____

_____

_____

_____

_____

Me: _____

_____

_____

_____

_____

Stonewalling:

You: _____

_____

_____

_____

_____

Me: _____

_____

_____

_____

_____

Pretending you understand:

You: _____

_____

_____

_____

_____

Me: _____

_____

_____

_____

_____

Expectations:

You: _____

_____

_____

_____

_____

Me: _____

_____

_____

_____

_____

LOVE AND RESPECT

Read Love and Respect, pages 26-31

» Do you have trouble thinking about what you're saying to your spouse before you speak it?

» Do you blurt things out and regret it later?

» Have you said something in the last couple months to your spouse that you regretted later?

» Do you truly want what is best for your spouse in life and in your marriage?

Do you believe your spouse always has the best intentions when it comes to things that affect you in life and marriage? Why or why not?

You: _____

_____

_____

_____

_____

Me: _____

_____

_____

_____

_____

» The next time you feel reactive, ask yourself these two questions:

* Will my spouse feel loved if I respond to them with these words?

* Will my spouse feel loved if I act on my impulse to just walk out the door?

» Communicating in love requires you to take a moment and respond, rather than react. It also requires you to be ready to make amends when you make mistakes. For some people, apologizing and promising to do better next time can be hard to do, but that gets easier with practice.

What are your top 2 love languages?

Go to www.5lovelanguages.com/profile/ to find out, if you have not already.

You: 1. _____ 2. _____

Me: 1. _____ 2. _____

How can you use your spouse's love language to show them love this week?

You: _____

_____

_____

_____

_____

Me: _____

_____

_____

_____

_____

What makes you feel loved by your spouse?

You: _____

_____

_____

_____

_____

Me: _____

_____

_____

_____

_____

What makes you feel unloved by your spouse?

You: _____

_____

_____

_____

_____

Me: _____

_____

_____

_____

_____

» Reflecting on each of your answers, can you see how you might have been missing the mark with your spouse's love language? If not, that's awesome! Now you know you are on the right track and can keep filling your spouse's love tank.

Do you respect your spouse?

You:	Yes	No
Me:	Yes	No

Explain your answer.

You: _____

_____

_____

_____

_____

Me: _____

_____

_____

_____

_____

Do you feel respected by your spouse?

You:	Yes	No
Me:	Yes	No

Explain your answer.

You: _____

_____

_____

_____

_____

Me: _____

_____

_____

_____

When do you feel the most respected by your spouse?

You: _____

_____

_____

_____

_____

Me: _____

_____

_____

_____

When do you feel disrespected by your spouse?

You: _____

_____

_____

_____

_____

Me: _____

_____

_____

_____

Do you feel safe in every way with your spouse?

You:	Yes	No
Me:	Yes	No

Explain your answer.

You: _____

_____

_____

_____

_____

Me: _____

_____

_____

_____

_____

How do you think a couple communicates with respect?

You: _____

_____

_____

_____

_____

Me: _____

_____

_____

_____

_____

What can you change in the way you communicate with your spouse
this week to be more respectful?

You: _____

_____

_____

_____

_____

Me: _____

_____

_____

_____

_____

Do you feel like you can give feedback to your spouse and it will be well received by them?

You:	Yes	No
Me:	Yes	No

Explain your answer.

You: _____

_____

_____

_____

_____

Me: _____

_____

_____

_____

_____

Do you feel you are open-minded when it comes to receiving feedback from your spouse?

You:	Yes	No
Me:	Yes	No

Explain your answer.

You: _____

_____

_____

_____

_____

Me: _____

_____

_____

_____

What is one thing you really want your spouse to work on improving this week?

You: _____

_____

_____

_____

_____

Me: _____

_____

_____

_____

» Will you agree to try and work on what your spouse has picked?

» We don't mean for you to give up the things you enjoy, but to be conscious of how your actions (or inactions) affect your spouse. You both decided to join your life together, and with that comes putting your spouse's needs above your wants. We encourage you to have a conversation about each area that you may not agree on and find a compromise using empathetic listening, which we cover later in chapter two.

Activity: Ask yourself before you say and do things this week, *"How would my spouse feel if I did this? Would my spouse feel respected and loved? How would I feel if they did this?"*

Chapter 2

Read How to Listen Effectively, pages 33-42

» What do you think about the statement we made in the beginning of the chapter, that the most vital part of communication is the art of listening? Do you agree or disagree?

» Can you think of a time recently that you were *inactively* listening to your spouse?

» Did you listen solely to give a reply or even interrupt your spouse?

What is your biggest struggle when it comes to *active* listening?

You: _____

_____

_____

_____

_____

Me: _____

_____

_____

_____

What can you do to implement *active* listening techniques in your marriage this week?

You: _____

_____

_____

_____

_____

Me: _____

_____

_____

_____

_____

» Three things we try to do to implement active listening is:

1) Say each other's name to get each other's attention.

2) Put the screens away so that our spouse can have our undivided attention.

3) Give each other a heads up when it comes to more involving conversations and find out which time is best to discuss it.

What makes you feel heard and understood when you communicate with your spouse?

You: _____

_____

_____

_____

_____

Me: _____

_____

_____

_____

_____

What distracts you from giving your undivided attention to your spouse?

You: _____

_____

_____

_____

_____

Me: _____

_____

_____

_____

_____

When do you feel you have your spouse's full attention?

You: _____

_____

_____

_____

_____

Me: _____

_____

_____

_____

_____

Describe what "giving your full attention" to your spouse means.

You: _____

_____

_____

_____

_____

Me: _____

_____

_____

_____

_____

How would you define *empathetic* listening?

You: _____

_____

_____

_____

_____

Me: _____

_____

_____

_____

_____

Do you think you listen to understand where your spouse is coming from,
with an open mind, the majority of the time?

| You: | Yes | No |

| Me: | Yes | No |

Do you think your spouse listens to understand where you are coming from,
with an open mind, the majority of the time?

| You: | Yes | No |

| Me: | Yes | No |

Do you find it difficult to actively try to understand and see where your spouse is coming
from, where they are, and why they feel the way they do?

| You: | Yes | No |

| Me: | Yes | No |

When it comes to *empathetic* listening, what is the most difficult part for you?

You: _____

_____

_____

_____

_____

Me: _____

_____

_____

_____

_____

» Three things we do to remain listening *empathetically*:

1) Take a break when we realize we are more reactive than responsive, or emotions are running high.

2) Curb negative thoughts by reminding ourselves that our spouse has the best intentions for us.

3) Remind our self that our spouse understands things differently and communicates differently as we try to focus on the message. Asking our self what is motivating our spouse to believe this way. What is the unspoken meaning?

What are some things you can do to implement *empathetic* listening in your communication this week?

You: _____

_____

_____

_____

_____

Me: _____

_____

_____

_____

_____

Do you believe everything in marriage has to be resolved?

You: Yes   No

Me: Yes   No

Do you believe you have to agree to disagree sometimes?

You: Yes   No

Me: Yes   No

What are some topics you believe must be resolved at all costs?

You: _____

_____

_____

_____

Me: _____

_____

_____

_____

What are some topics you believe are fine to agree to disagree on?

You: _____

_____

_____

_____

_____

Me: _____

_____

_____

_____

_____

When practicing empathetic listening, you will both have the opportunity to explain why you feel so strongly about your opinions.

» When you vent to your spouse, do you let them know that you just want them to listen and sympathize with you?

» If you need a solution, do you ask for one or just start talking and get upset when they don't read your mind and help you?

Activity: Share some words of encouragement to your spouse right now verbally, or write a letter if that is easier for you.

How to Listen to Your Spouse

Read How to Listen to Your Spouse, pages 42-44

When do you feel you have your spouse's full attention?

You: _____

_____

_____

_____

_____

Me: _____

_____

_____

_____

_____

What distracts you from giving your undivided attention to your spouse?

You: _____

_____

_____

_____

_____

Me: _____

_____

_____

_____

_____

Do you find it difficult to listen calmly when your spouse is angry at you or someone else, upset from a loss, frustrated, or just having a bad day? If so, why?

You: _____

_____

_____

_____

_____

Me: _____

_____

_____

_____

Do you find it uncomfortable when your spouse cries? If so, why?

You: _____

_____

_____

_____

_____

Me: _____

_____

_____

_____

_____

Do you have trouble expressing emotions to your spouse? If so, why?

You: _____

_____

_____

_____

Me: _____

_____

_____

_____

Are you able to ask how your spouse is feeling when you communicate? If not, why?

You: _____

_____

_____

_____

_____

Me: _____

_____

_____

_____

We talked about telling your spouse what you need from them, such as listening to you vent or help find a solution, in the previous section. But what can you do when your spouse doesn't let you know what they need?

_____

_____

_____

_____

_____

_____

_____

_____

» We ask a simple question: "Would you like my opinion, or do you just want me to listen?"

Do you value your spouse's opinions and input in every area of your marriage? Why?

You: _____

_____

_____

_____

_____

Me: _____

_____

_____

_____

_____

A Few Tools to Communicate Better

Read A Few Tools to Communicate Better, pages 44-50

In this section of chapter two, we went over some tips you can implement in your conversations to help you communicate more efficiently with each other. Below each tool, write down specific ways you will start using them in how you communicate with your spouse this week. It may help to add ways you can help remind each other when you notice the other is veering off into your old communication patterns.

Get to the point.

_____

_____

_____

_____

_____

Stay on topic.

_____

_____

_____

_____

_____

Choose a good time.

_____

_____

_____

_____

_____

Have an open mind.

_____

_____

_____

_____

Take a break.

_____

_____

_____

_____

Listen with empathy.

_____

_____

_____

_____

Clarify.

_____

_____

_____

_____

Speak their language.

_____

_____

_____

_____

_____

Use body language.

_____

_____

_____

_____

_____

Pay attention.

_____

_____

_____

_____

_____

Be aware of your tone and mindful of your word choice.

_____

_____

_____

_____

_____

Win together.

_____

_____

_____

_____

_____

Which communication tool listed in this chapter will you implement first?

_____

_____

CHAPTER 3

Read Emotional Intelligence for Better Conversations, pages 53-57

What does emotional intelligence mean to you?

You: _____

_____

_____

_____

_____

Me: _____

_____

_____

_____

_____

Where do you feel you are when it comes to emotional intelligence on a scale of 1-10?

You: 1   2   3   4   5   6   7   8   9   10

Me: 1   2   3   4   5   6   7   8   9   10

Where do you feel your spouse is when it comes to emotional intelligence on a scale of 1-10?

You: 1   2   3   4   5   6   7   8   9   10

Me: 1   2   3   4   5   6   7   8   9   10

Do you agree that emotional intelligence is an intangible asset that will aid you in moving forward in your career, your marriage, and your life? Why?

You: _____

_____

_____

_____

_____

Me: _____

_____

_____

_____

_____

Do you take ownership of your emotions instead of blaming your spouse?

You: Yes   No

Me: Yes   No

Do you agree with your spouse's answer? Why?

You: _____

_____

_____

_____

_____

Me: _____

_____

_____

_____

_____

Do you believe that in order to have better communication in your marriage, you both have to change some behaviors that are not beneficial? Why?

You: _____

_____

_____

_____

_____

Me: _____

_____

_____

_____

_____

What will you do this week to grow your emotional intelligence as an individual?

You: _____

_____

_____

_____

_____

Me: _____

_____

_____

_____

_____

What are some things you can do when you are triggered to try and calm your body down? What are some things your spouse can do to help you?

You: _____

_____

_____

_____

_____

Me: _____

_____

_____

_____

_____

» Things we suggest are: physically trying to move and engage your body with a short walk, get a drink, or ask yourself if the trigger would matter in five minutes, an hour, the next day, or six months from now.

How will you help prepare your spouse for the bigger or more involving conversations?

You: _____

_____

_____

_____

_____

Me: _____

_____

_____

_____

_____

WHY PATIENCE IS YOUR FRIEND

Read Why Patience is Your Friend, pages 57-63

How do you feel you rate on the patience scale of 1-10? Do you agree with your spouse?

You: 1   2   3   4   5   6   7   8   9   10

Me: 1   2   3   4   5   6   7   8   9   10

What can you do to have more patience with your spouse?

You: _____

_____

_____

_____

_____

Me: _____

_____

_____

_____

Can you think of a time you lost your patience with your spouse? What was the trigger? What was the root of what set you off?

You: _____

_____

_____

_____

_____

Me: _____

_____

_____

_____

_____

How can you do better next time?

You: _____

_____

_____

_____

_____

Me: _____

_____

_____

_____

_____

How will you specifically commit to implementing the tools below in your marriage to help you grow your patience?

Limit technology.

You: _____

_____

_____

_____

_____

Me: _____

_____

_____

_____

_____

Practice meditation.

You: _____

_____

_____

_____

_____

Me: _____

_____

_____

_____

_____

Manage your expectations.

You: _____

_____

_____

_____

_____

Me: _____

_____

_____

_____

_____

Practice emotional intelligence.

You: _____

_____

_____

_____

_____

Me: _____

_____

_____

_____

_____

Choose your timing well.

You: _____

_____

_____

_____

_____

Me: _____

_____

_____

_____

_____

How will you create a safe place in your marriage where you both feel at ease talking to one another about absolutely everything and anything?

_____

_____

_____

_____

_____

_____

_____

_____

_____

_____

Embracing Gratitude

Read Embracing Gratitude, pages 63-64

Write down 10 things you are grateful for about your spouse.
Take notice how easy or difficult this exercise is.

You:

1. _____
2. _____
3. _____
4. _____
5. _____
6. _____
7. _____
8. _____
9. _____
10. _____

Me:

1. _____
2. _____
3. _____
4. _____
5. _____
6. _____
7. _____

8. _____

9. _____

10. _____

» Does the feeling of gratitude towards your spouse come naturally for you?

» How often do you thank each other for the little things?

How will you incorporate more gratitude in the coming weeks?

You: _____

_____

_____

_____

_____

Me: _____

_____

_____

_____

_____

Activity: Create a new habit of thanking each other in some form at least once a day.

CHAPTER 4

Read It's Not Possible Without Trust, pages 67-76

Do you trust your spouse completely?

You:	Yes	No	Mostly
Me:	Yes	No	Mostly

Are you truly open and honest with your spouse about everything?

You:	Yes	No	Mostly
Me:	Yes	No	Mostly

What are some of the areas, or times, that are harder for you to tell the
whole truth to your spouse?

You: _____

_____

_____

_____

_____

Me: _____

_____

_____

_____

_____

What are a few things your spouse does that makes you feel like you *can't* trust them in certain areas?

You: _____

_____

_____

_____

_____

Me: _____

_____

_____

_____

_____

What are some things your spouse does that makes you feel like you *can* trust them?

You: _____

_____

_____

_____

_____

Me: _____

_____

_____

_____

_____

What are 3 trust boundaries that, if your spouse crossed them, there would be no coming back from?

You:

1. _____

2. _____

3. _____

Me:

1. _____

2. _____

3. _____

Do you feel like you know your spouse inside and out?

You: Yes   No   Mostly

You: Yes   No   Mostly

Do you feel like your spouse knows you inside and out?

You: Yes   No   Mostly

Me: Yes   No   Mostly

Do you have anything you haven't told your spouse about from your past?

You: Yes   No

Me: Yes   No

What about your present?

You: Yes   No

Me: Yes   No

What about your future plans?

You:	Yes	No
Me:	Yes	No

Is there a question you have been wanting to ask your spouse for some time?

You:	Yes	No
Me:	Yes	No

» If you circled yes, take the time now to discuss the question(s).

In your opinion, can one little white lie really do much harm to a marriage?

You:	Yes	No
Me:	Yes	No

What about lying by omission?

You:	Yes	No
Me:	Yes	No

Do you both agree to make open honesty a priority in your marriage, even when it is tough?

You:	Yes	No
Me:	Yes	No

Do you both agree to carefully express when you need to see improvement in the way your spouse is communicating with you?

You:	Yes	No
Me:	Yes	No

When your spouse verbalizes these needs to you, do you agree to do your best and take action to improve your communication with them?

You:	Yes	No
Me:	Yes	No

Is there any area in your life where you were not completely honest with your spouse in the past that you feel you should bring to light now?

You:	Yes	No
Me:	Yes	No

» Is there any area in your marriage you feel that you owe your spouse a sincere apology for? Now is your time.

Do you feel like your spouse stands by their word and is good at keeping promises?

You:	Yes	No
Me:	Yes	No

Explain your answer.

You: _____

_____

_____

_____

Me: _____

_____

_____

_____

_____

What can you do when it is difficult to understand, or be interested in,
what your spouse wants to share with you?

You: _____

_____

_____

_____

_____

Me: _____

_____

_____

_____

_____

What can you each do to nurture and protect the trust you have built,
or are building, in your marriage?

_____

_____

_____

_____

_____

_____

_____

_____

_____

_____

» Go over the Tips for Cultivating Trust in Your Marriage on pages 75-76.

Activity: Do you connect every day and have conversations about your daily activities, struggles, and what you're learning about for at least an hour? Carve out time every day – starting today – to just sit together and have a conversation!

BUILDING A SAFE ENVIRONMENT

Read Building a Safe Environment, pages 76-79

Is it hard for you to verbalize your feelings and emotions to your spouse?

You:	Yes	No
Me:	Yes	No

Explain your answer.

You: _____

_____

_____

_____

_____

Me: _____

_____

_____

_____

_____

Which emotions are the hardest for you to verbalize to your spouse?

You: _____

_____

_____

_____

_____

Me: _____

_____

_____

_____

_____

Do you keep your feelings hidden about anything from your spouse? Which ones, and why?

You: _____

_____

_____

_____

_____

Me: _____

_____

_____

_____

_____

Pay attention to your feelings when you think about sitting down with your spouse and having a conversation. Do you dread all your conversations or just certain ones? Why do you think that is?

You: _____

_____

_____

_____

_____

Me: _____

_____

_____

_____

_____

When was a time, more recently, you felt heard and empathized by your spouse?

You: _____

_____

_____

_____

_____

Me: _____

_____

_____

_____

_____

What does a safe environment look like to you, where you would feel comfortable being vulnerable enough to share your innermost thoughts and emotions?

You: _____

_____

_____

_____

_____

Me: _____

_____

_____

_____

_____

Is there anything that is hindering a safe environment from happening?

You: _____

_____

_____

_____

_____

Me: _____

_____

_____

_____

_____

Do you feel your spouse is there for you when you need them?

You: _____

_____

_____

_____

_____

Me: _____

_____

_____

_____

_____

What can your spouse do to show you that they are there for you?

You: _____

_____

_____

_____

_____

Me: _____

_____

_____

_____

_____

Using the sandwich technique we talked about on page 78, find a time with your spouse to offer a helpful critique, mixed in with two compliments.

After making sure you and your spouse are relaxed and ready to listen with an open mind and empathy, take turns completing these sentences:

You: Honey, I am very happy with how you have helped/grown/put in effort to

_____.

I have just noticed that sometimes you may

_____.

I know you are not doing this to

(_____ emotion) me, but I feel

_____ when this happens.

Could you try to do more/less/stop?

Me: Honey, I am very happy with how you have helped/grown/put in effort to

_____.

I have just noticed that sometimes you may

_____.

I know you are not doing this to

(_____ emotion) me, but I feel

_____ when this happens.

Could you try to do more/less/stop?

Do you feel that you can go to your spouse, without judgement, when you make mistakes or just need them to listen to what is going on with you?

You: Yes   No

Me: Yes   No

Explain your answer.

You: _____

_____

_____

_____

_____

Me: _____

_____

_____

_____

Do you feel like you are blamed unfairly by your spouse sometimes?

You: Yes   No

Me: Yes   No

Do you feel accepted by your spouse in every way? If not, how can you work towards that?

You: _____

_____

_____

_____

_____

Me: _____

_____

_____

_____

_____

What can you do this week to put what you have learned in this section to work in your marriage?

You: _____

_____

_____

_____

_____

Me: _____

_____

_____

_____

_____

Activity: Come up with a plan and take steps, together, to create the ideal marriage relationship where you both feel safe enough to be vulnerable.

THE VALUE OF MARRIAGE CHECK-UPS

Read The Value of Marriage Check-ups, pages 79-82

What does a marriage check-up mean to you?

You: _____

_____

_____

_____

_____

Me: _____

_____

_____

_____

_____

Would you be open to having a weekly marriage check-up, or at a frequency you both agree on?

You:	Yes	No
Me:	Yes	No

What scares you about having a marriage check-up?

You: _____

_____

_____

_____

_____

Me: _____

_____

_____

_____

What ground rules will you set up before you have your first check-up?

1. _____

2. _____

3. _____

4. _____

5. _____

6. _____

7. _____

8. _____

9. _____

10. _____

» Talk about the different areas of your marriage: friendship (and fun), emotional, intellectual, sexual, and anything else you feel is important.

What do you feel is the strongest area in your marriage?

_____

Why?

_____

_____

_____

_____

Rate the state of these areas on a scale of 1 to 10, and then ask each other what you could do to make it better. What is missing? Ask these questions for each of the different areas, and come up with a plan to improve. If there is more than one thing to work on, decide together on the most important improvement needed for each of you, and start there. You are basically asking, "Are your needs met? How can I meet your needs better? How can I make your life better?"

How happy are you with the emotional intimacy in your marriage?

You:	1	2	3	4	5	6	7	8	9	10
Me:	1	2	3	4	5	6	7	8	9	10

What can we each do individually, or together, to improve this area?

You: _____

_____

_____

_____

_____

Me: _____

_____

_____

_____

_____

How happy are you with the friendship and fun activities in your marriage?

You: 1   2   3   4   5   6   7   8   9   10

Me: 1   2   3   4   5   6   7   8   9   10

What can we each do individually, or together, to improve this area?

You: _____

_____

_____

_____

_____

Me: _____

_____

_____

_____

_____

How happy are you with the intellectual intimacy in your marriage?

You: 1   2   3   4   5   6   7   8   9   10

Me: 1   2   3   4   5   6   7   8   9   10

What can we each do individually, or together, to improve this area?

You: _____

_____

_____

_____

_____

Me: _____

_____

_____

_____

How happy are you with the sexual intimacy in your marriage?

You:	1	2	3	4	5	6	7	8	9	10
Me:	1	2	3	4	5	6	7	8	9	10

What can we each do individually, or together, to improve this area?

You: _____

_____

_____

_____

_____

Me: _____

_____

_____

_____

_____

How happy are you with the way finances are handled in your marriage?

You: 1   2   3   4   5   6   7   8   9   10

Me: 1   2   3   4   5   6   7   8   9   10

What can we each do individually, or together, to improve this area?

You: _____

_____

_____

_____

_____

Me: _____

_____

_____

_____

_____

Activity: Schedule a weekly marriage check-up on your calendar.

CHAPTER 5

Read How to Communicate Through Difficult Emotions, pages 85-91

How do you think communicating about your emotions will enhance your intimacy?

You: _____

_____

_____

_____

_____

Me: _____

_____

_____

_____

_____

When you feel hurt by your spouse, how do you handle it?

You: _____

_____

_____

_____

_____

Me: _____

_____

_____

_____

Do you feel any resentment towards your spouse?

You:	Yes	No
Me:	Yes	No

If so, is it because of deeper needs that you did not communicate, such as expectations, feeling unappreciated, etc.?

You: _____

_____

_____

_____

_____

Me: _____

_____

_____

_____

_____

What is the one thing you have argued about the most in the past ninety days?

You: _____

_____

_____

_____

_____

Me: _____

_____

_____

_____

_____

What do you think is the root cause, and how can it be resolved?

You: _____

_____

_____

_____

_____

Me: _____

_____

_____

_____

_____

Do you take responsibility for your own emotions?

You: Yes   No

Me: Yes   No

Do you feel you spouse takes responsibility for their own emotions?

You: Yes   No

Me: Yes   No

Are you open with your spouse about your worries and fears?

You: Yes   No

Me: Yes   No

If not, why?

You: _____

_____

_____

_____

_____

Me: _____

_____

_____

_____

_____

Do you think your spouse sees you as weak?

You: Yes   No

Me: Yes   No

Are you afraid of your spouse seeing you as weak?

You: Yes   No

Me: Yes   No

How can your spouse help you communicate the more challenging
emotions you have with them?

You: _____

_____

_____

_____

_____

Me: _____

_____

_____

_____

_____

Are you willing to do put these ideas in place to help your spouse
communicate better with you?

You: Yes   No

Me: Yes   No

» For the next exercise, if verbalizing certain things is too much at this point, one handy tool that can help you is writing a letter to each other. Whether this letter is to express intentions, appreciation, affection, or frustration, it can be a baby step to some of these harder-to-express emotions. Be sure to give your spouse the opportunity to respond.

» Have discussions with open-ended questions. "What was that like? How did that feel? Who, what, when, why, and how?" Always go into the conversation assuming you have something to learn from your spouse, and be willing to set aside yourself and your personal opinions. This opens you up for new insights and growth, as well as communicating acceptance to your spouse.

Take turns filling in the blanks.

You:

What makes you feel stressed?

_____

_____

_____

_____

_____

What makes you frustrated with your spouse?

_____

_____

_____

_____

_____

What makes you feel frustrated at your job?

_____

_____

_____

_____

_____

What makes you feel stressed with your family?

_____

_____

_____

_____

_____

How do you feel when your spouse does/doesn't do

_____

_____

_____

_____

_____

What is your biggest fear in your marriage?

_____

_____

_____

_____

_____

What are some other things you are afraid of?

_____

_____

_____

_____

_____

What makes you sad in your marriage?

_____

_____

_____

_____

_____

What makes you feel lonely in your marriage?

_____

_____

_____

_____

_____

What makes you feel the happiest in your marriage?

_____

_____

_____

_____

_____

What makes you feel like the best spouse in the world?

_____

_____

_____

_____

_____

Me:

What makes you feel stressed?

_____

_____

_____

_____

_____

What makes you frustrated with your spouse?

_____

_____

_____

_____

_____

What makes you feel frustrated at your job?

_____

_____

_____

_____

_____

What makes you feel stressed with your family?

_____

_____

_____

_____

How do you feel when your spouse does/doesn't do

_____

_____

_____

_____

What is your biggest fear in your marriage?

_____

_____

_____

_____

What are some other things you are afraid of?

_____

_____

_____

_____

What makes you sad in your marriage?

_____

_____

_____

_____

_____

What makes you feel lonely in your marriage?

_____

_____

_____

_____

_____

What makes you feel the happiest in your marriage?

_____

_____

_____

_____

_____

What makes you feel like the best spouse in the world?

_____

_____

_____

_____

_____

How do you handle conflict with your in-laws?

You: _____

_____

_____

_____

_____

Me: _____

_____

_____

_____

What can you do, as a couple, to improve the way you handle conflict with your in-laws?

_____

_____

_____

_____

_____

If you were to go through one of the following in your marriage, write down what you would need and expect from your spouse as you react to each event.

Unexpected pregnancy

You: _____

_____

_____

_____

_____

Me: _____

_____

_____

_____

_____

Loss of a child

You: _____

_____

_____

_____

Me: _____

_____

_____

_____

_____

Loss of a job

You: _____

_____

_____

_____

_____

Me: _____

_____

_____

_____

_____

House foreclosure

You: _____

_____

_____

_____

_____

Me: _____

_____

_____

_____

_____

Major illness of yourself

You: _____

_____

_____

_____

_____

Me: _____

_____

_____

_____

_____

Major illness of a child

You: _____

_____

_____

_____

_____

Me: _____

_____

_____

_____

_____

**Having to live in a smaller house or apartment longer than you wish,
or not being able to buy a house**

You: _____

_____

_____

_____

_____

Me: _____

_____

_____

_____

_____

Your spouse quitting their job to start their own business

You: _____

_____

_____

_____

_____

Me: _____

_____

_____

_____

_____

Your spouse wishing to be a stay-at-home parent

You: _____

_____

_____

_____

_____

Me: _____

_____

_____

_____

_____

Your spouse not wanting to be a stay-at-home parent

You: _____

_____

_____

_____

_____

Me: _____

_____

_____

_____

Infertility

You: _____

_____

_____

_____

Me: _____

_____

_____

_____

Your spouse not wanting to have children at all

You: _____

_____

_____

_____

Me: _____

_____

_____

_____

_____

Your spouse not wanting to have any more children, or have an abortion

You: _____

_____

_____

_____

Me: _____

_____

_____

_____

Your spouse having contact with old flames or people they may be attracted to

You: _____

_____

_____

_____

_____

Me: _____

_____

_____

_____

Your spouse being attracted to another person

You: _____

_____

_____

_____

_____

Me: _____

_____

_____

_____

Spouse loses, or changes, their religion

You: _____

_____

_____

_____

_____

Me: _____

_____

_____

_____

_____

Spouse confides in you that they have an addiction

You: _____

_____

_____

_____

_____

Me: _____

_____

_____

_____

_____

HOW EFFECTIVELY COMMUNICATING YOUR EMOTIONS IMPROVES INTIMACY

Read How Effectively Communicating Your Emotions Improves Intimacy, pages 91-93

Can you see how you communicate differently with other people than you do with your spouse? List one example.

You: _____

_____

_____

_____

_____

Me: _____

_____

_____

_____

_____

» Conversation starters can help get the ball rolling and allow you to learn things about each other on a continuous basis. That constant learning about each other will enhance your communication and your intimacy, which goes hand in hand.

Take some time and have a conversation with some of these conversation starters.

1) How do you feel most connected in our friendship?

   ◦ How can we strengthen our friendship?

2) When do you feel emotionally connected to me?

3) How do your parents communicate?

- What do you like about how they communicate?

- What don't you like about it?

- How do you communicate like them?

- How do you communicate differently from them?

4) Do you feel like you are getting enough time to spend with your friends and family? If no, what can we do to increase it without negatively impacting our relationship?

5) Tell me about a challenge you've had in your life.

- What are you grateful for from experiencing that hardship, and what did you learn?

6) How would you like to start your ideal morning?

7) Have you ever felt rejected by me?

- What did I do or say that made you feel rejected?

8) What are some ways you like to socially interact with me?

9) What have you been interested in or learning about lately?

10) What are five things you love about me?

11) When you talk about me with someone, do you have positive, negative, or neutral things to say?

- What kind of feelings do you get when you think or talk about me?

12) What is your favorite memory of our wedding day?

- What about our wedding night?

13) Which married couple do you look up to the most, and why?

14) How do you feel the most connected physically to me?

- How do you want to be touched non-sexually?

- What is one way I can make an effort this week to enhance that physical connection between us?

15) What is one thing you discovered about me after we got married that you love?

- What is one thing that you discovered about me after we got married that you dislike?

16) What are the top five things you appreciate about me?

17) How would you describe our relationship in three words?

18) What is better than amazing sex?

19) What is a question about life that you wish you had the answer to?

20) What were the highest points of your life?

- What did you learn through those times?

21) What were the highest points of our relationship?

- The most difficult?

- What did you each learn through those times?

22) What is your first memory of me? Describe it in as much detail as you can remember.

23) How can we make our relationship affair-proof?

24) How can we communicate better?

25) What does your ideal career look like?

26) Do you ever feel controlled by me?

27) What does your ideal life look like? Give specific details.

28) What do you want the atmosphere in our home to feel like?

29) What does the best relationship possible look like to you?

- What is our relationship missing to be that great?

- What can we do to work towards that kind of relationship?

30) Have you ever saved someone's life?

- Has anyone ever saved your life?

31) What person (or people) had the most impact on your life, and how?

32) What do you do to get yourself in a better mood when you are not feeling great?

33) What book has influenced your life the most?

34) How would you feel if I changed my religious beliefs?

35) Do you feel unworthy of my love?

36) How do you feel about supporting family members financially?

   ◦ What if one or more of your parents needed to be taken care of?

   ◦ Would you want them to live with you?

   ◦ What if it was another family member that needed a full-time caregiver?

37) What makes you attracted to me physically?

   ◦ Emotionally?

   ◦ Intellectually?

   ◦ Spiritually?

38) How do you feel the closest connection with me in these roles:

   ◦ As an individual

   ◦ Partner or spouse

   ◦ Parent

   ◦ What is one way we can improve our relationship connection in these areas this week?

39) What brings you the most joy in our relationship?

40) What are you dreading in life right now?

41) What is something you have struggled with your entire life?

   ◦ Does anyone know about it?

   ◦ Why do you think you struggle with it?

   ◦ Have you overcome it? If so, how did you overcome it?

42) What are the most important skills you learned from your parents?

43) What are three physical shows of affection you really enjoy from me and you wish I would do more often?

44) Do you have trouble opening up and talking to me about anything?

  ◦ Do you find it difficult feeling intimate with me in any form?

  ◦ Are you worried about being hurt?

  ◦ Are there any secrets you have not told me?

  ◦ Is there any subject that you feel is too personal to talk to me about?

  ◦ What is something about you that you feel I don't need to know? Why?

  ◦ What makes you not want to talk to me?

45) If you had to be on life support, would you want to continue to be kept alive?

  ◦ What if you had no brain activity?

  ◦ What if you were paralyzed?

  ◦ What if you needed life support machines to remain alive for the rest of your life?

  ◦ What if you were in a coma?

46) How do you feel the most connected to me intellectually?

  ◦ What is one thing we can do this week to deepen that intimacy?

47) How do you feel the most spiritually connected with me?

  ◦ What is one thing we can do this week to deepen that connection?

For more conversation starters, check out our book *Questions for Couples: 469 Thought-Provoking Conversation Starters for Connecting, Building Trust, and Rekindling Intimacy.*

Sexpectations

Read Sexpectations, pages 93-96

What are some sexpectations that you have?

You: _____

_____

_____

_____

_____

Me: _____

_____

_____

_____

_____

What is the minimum number of times you want to have sex every week?

You: _____

Me: _____

What is the maximum?

You: _____

Me: _____

What is a number you can compromise on?

_____

What is one place you would like to have sex with your spouse but have not yet?

You: _____

Me: _____

What makes you uncomfortable when talking about sex?

You: _____

_____

_____

_____

_____

Me: _____

_____

_____

_____

_____

How do you feel after you have sex?

You: _____

_____

_____

_____

_____

Me: _____

_____

_____

_____

_____

What would you like to do right after sex?

You: _____

_____

_____

_____

_____

Me: _____

_____

_____

_____

_____

Do you ever feel dirty or ashamed after having sex with your spouse?

You:	Yes	No	Sometimes
Me:	Yes	No	Sometimes

Do you feel safe sexually with your spouse?

You:	Yes	No	Sometimes
Me:	Yes	No	Sometimes

What sex acts do you find off-limits or consider gross?

You: _____

_____

_____

_____

_____

Me: _____

_____

_____

_____

Where are the spots that drive you crazy in a good way during sex?

You: _____

_____

_____

_____

_____

Me: _____

_____

_____

_____

Where are the places that drive you crazy in a bad way during sex?

You: _____

_____

_____

_____

_____

Me: _____

_____

_____

_____

Which part of your body would you like to be paid more attention to during sex?

You: _____

_____

_____

_____

_____

Me: _____

_____

_____

_____

_____

What do you need to be in the mood for sex?

You: _____

_____

_____

_____

_____

Me: _____

_____

_____

_____

What gets you in the mood/ turns you on sexually?

You: _____

_____

_____

_____

_____

Me: _____

_____

_____

_____

_____

What turns you off sexually?

You: _____

_____

_____

_____

_____

Me: _____

_____

_____

_____

_____

Do you think your spouse should have sex with you even when they are not in the mood?

You:	Yes	No	Sometimes
Me:	Yes	No	Sometimes

Do you communicate with your spouse before sex about what kind of sex you are in the mood for? Example: Quickie, rough, slow, specific positions, toys to use, etc.

You:	Yes	No	Sometimes
Me:	Yes	No	Sometimes

Do you communicate with your spouse during sex about what you like, areas to avoid, places to spend more time exploring, etc.?

You:	Yes	No	Sometimes
Me:	Yes	No	Sometimes

Do you feel it would be helpful to mark down on the calendar when you both agree to have sex, so each of you has time to prepare your mind and body?

| You: | Yes | No | Sometimes |
| You: | Yes | No | Sometimes |

Do you want to take turns initiating sex?

| You: | Yes | No | Sometimes |
| Me: | Yes | No | Sometimes |

If yes, how will you take turns initiating sex?

_____

_____

_____

_____

_____

_____

_____

How do you usually initiate sex?

You: _____

_____

_____

_____

_____

Me: _____

_____

_____

_____

_____

What is something you want to do more of, or something new you want to explore, when it comes to sex?

You: _____

_____

_____

_____

_____

Me: _____

_____

_____

_____

_____

What is something you want to do less of when it comes to sex?

You: _____

_____

_____

_____

_____

Me: _____

_____

_____

_____

_____

» Do you have conversations sometimes after sex about what you enjoyed and how it made you feel?

Take time to think back to the last time you had sex and fill in the blank.

You: I had a lot of fun making love with you last night. Especially when you touched my/did _____ and gave it all your attention. I felt so turned on and sexy when you did that.

Me: I had a lot of fun making love with you last night. Especially when you touched my/did _____ and gave it all your attention. I felt so turned on and sexy when you did that.

What makes you feel sexy?

You: _____

_____

_____

_____

_____

Me: _____

_____

_____

_____

_____

Remember to be kind with your words and focus on the positive.

You: I love it when you/we _____

_____

_____

_____. Let's do more of that.

Me: I love it when you/we _____

_____

_____

_____. Let's do more of that.

How do you view sex? What is its purpose?

You: _____

_____

_____

_____

_____

Me: _____

_____

_____

_____

_____

How do you feel about sex?

You: _____

_____

_____

_____

_____

Me: _____

_____

_____

_____

Are there any sexual boundaries you have or want to create with your spouse?

You: _____

_____

_____

_____

_____

Me: _____

_____

_____

_____

What makes you uncomfortable when it comes to sex?

You: _____

_____

_____

_____

Me: _____

_____

_____

_____

What is one of your fantasies?

You: _____

_____

_____

_____

Me: _____

_____

_____

_____

When your spouse tells you they are not in the mood to have sex with you,
how does that make you feel? Why?

You: _____

_____

_____

_____

_____

Me: _____

_____

_____

_____

_____

Do you feel like there is enough romance in your marriage?

You:	Yes	No
Me:	Yes	No

What is romantic to you?

You: _____

_____

_____

_____

_____

Me: _____

_____

_____

_____

_____

WHEN MONEY BECOMES AN ISSUE

Read When Money Becomes an Issue, pages 97-99

What makes it hard for you to communicate with your spouse about money?

You: _____

_____

_____

_____

_____

Me: _____

_____

_____

_____

_____

Who is the saver, and who is the spender?

You: _____

Me: _____

How do you think talking about your money will help your marriage?

You: _____

_____

_____

_____

_____

Me: _____

_____

_____

_____

_____

Why is agreeing on finances important for your you, your marriage, and your family?

You: _____

_____

_____

_____

_____

Me: _____

_____

_____

_____

_____

Do you think it works better to share money accounts/credit cards
or keep them separately? Why?

You: _____

_____

_____

_____

_____

Me: _____

_____

_____

_____

_____

What are some of your individual financial goals?

You: _____

_____

_____

_____

_____

Me: _____

_____

_____

_____

_____

What are some of your financial goals as a couple?
If you have not made any, take this time to do so.

_____

_____

_____

_____

_____

_____

_____

What expectations do you have when it comes to money, finances, income,
paying bills, loans, debt, etc.?

You: _____

_____

_____

_____

Me: _____

_____

_____

_____

Do you think having an emergency fund is a good idea?
If so, what amount should you keep in that fund?

_____

Out of the two of you, who is better at handling money?

_____

What makes you feel stressed when dealing with financial issues,
and how do you deal with that stress?

You: _____

_____

_____

_____

_____

Me: _____

_____

_____

_____

_____

What is one worry you have had about your money and finances in the past thirty days?

You: _____

_____

_____

_____

_____

Me: _____

_____

_____

_____

How can I help you to overcome this frustration or stress?

You: _____

_____

_____

_____

Me: _____

_____

_____

_____

How should we prepare for a financial emergency?

You: _____

_____

_____

_____

Me: _____

_____

_____

_____

What circumstances are you okay with going into debt for?

You: _____

_____

_____

_____

_____

Me: _____

_____

_____

_____

_____

How do you feel about paying off debt?

You: _____

_____

_____

_____

_____

Me: _____

_____

_____

_____

_____

Should we create a plan for paying off our debt?

You:	Yes	No
Me:	Yes	No

How do you feel about lending money to family members?

You: _____

_____

_____

_____

_____

Me: _____

_____

_____

_____

_____

How much would you be comfortable with?

You: _____

Me: _____

What if we do loan them money and they do not pay it back?

You: _____

_____

_____

_____

_____

Me: _____

_____

_____

_____

_____

What about loaning money to friends?

You: _____

_____

_____

_____

_____

Me: _____

_____

_____

_____

_____

Do you think budgeting together will benefit your marriage?

You:	Yes	No
Me:	Yes	No

Activity: Start with creating a monthly budget together. Then, once you feel you have that down, create a list of all the events and bigger expenses throughout the year that you need to be prepared for. By doing this, you will have the conversations that keep you grounded and on track to achieve your financial goals together.

CHAPTER 6

Read How to Communicate Through Conflict, pages 101-106

Do you both agree that in your marriage both of you have equal rights and responsibilities?

You:	Yes	No
Me:	Yes	No

Do you agree that your opinions matter equally?

You:	Yes	No
Me:	Yes	No

What expectations do you have when it comes to arguing with your spouse?

You: _____

_____

_____

_____

_____

Me: _____

_____

_____

_____

_____

What are some examples of disagreements you witnessed growing up? How did your parents or caretakers deal with conflict?

You: _____

_____

_____

_____

_____

Me: _____

_____

_____

_____

How are you like/unlike them, pertaining to disagreements?

You: _____

_____

_____

_____

_____

Me: _____

_____

_____

_____

» After reflecting on these similarities and differences, take some time to discuss which parts you wish to continue and which parts you want to discontinue in your marriage.

Can you recognize any of the Four Horseman that Dr. Gottman talks about in the way you argue with your spouse? Circle which ones you each use.

You:	Criticism	Contempt	Defensiveness	Stonewalling
Me:	Criticism	Contempt	Defensiveness	Stonewalling

Do you or your spouse ever use terms like: "you never" or "you always"?

You:	Yes	No
Me:	Yes	No

When you feel yourself, or your spouse, starting to use *criticism* in your arguments, what can you do to respectfully draw each other's attention to it so that you can avoid this pitfall?

_____

_____

_____

_____

_____

_____

_____

When you feel yourself, or your spouse, starting to use *contempt* in your arguments, what can you do to respectfully draw each other's attention to it so that you can avoid this pitfall?

_____

_____

_____

_____

_____

_____

When you feel yourself, or your spouse, starting to use *defensiveness* in your arguments, what can you do to respectfully draw each other's attention to it so that you can avoid this pitfall?

_____

_____

_____

_____

_____

_____

_____

When you feel yourself, or your spouse, starting to *stonewall* during your arguments, what can you do to respectfully draw each other's attention to it so that you can avoid this pitfall?

_____

_____

_____

_____

_____

_____

_____

_____

TIPS FOR COMMUNICATING THROUGH CONFLICT

Read Tips for Communicating Through Conflict, pages 106-109

Write down how you will implement the following tips in the next disagreement you have with your spouse.

How will you **set the tone** for your disagreements and make sure that your voices and words remain calm and respectful?

You: _____

_____

_____

_____

_____

Me: _____

_____

_____

_____

_____

How will you **prepare your spouse** for a more involved conversation?

You: _____

_____

_____

_____

_____

Me: _____

_____

_____

_____

_____

How will you **avoid criticism** while disagreeing?

You: _____

_____

_____

_____

_____

Me: _____

_____

_____

_____

_____

How will you each **avoid becoming defensive?**

You: _____

_____

_____

_____

_____

Me: _____

_____

_____

_____

_____

How will you each **have patience** while communicating with your spouse?

You: _____

_____

_____

_____

_____

Me: _____

_____

_____

_____

_____

How will you let your spouse **know your expectations** and remain aware of them yourself?

You: _____

_____

_____

_____

_____

Me: _____

_____

_____

_____

_____

Activity: What are 3 things you can do this week to communicate peacefully through any conflict that arises?

1. _____

2. _____

3. _____

Resolving Your Differences

Read Resolving Your Differences, pages 109-114

Do you agree that, ultimately, you want the best for your spouse, which, in turn, works out to be the best for both of you as a unit?

You:	Yes	No
Me:	Yes	No

Do you both agree to try and remember to give your spouse the same amount of respect you desire, and *treat them the way you want to be treated*?

You:	Yes	No
Me:	Yes	No

Do you agree to accept your spouse's influence on your life and decisions?

You:	Yes	No
Me:	Yes	No

Are you open to learning from your spouse?

You:	Yes	No
Me:	Yes	No

How soon do you want to resolve a conflict with your spouse, ideally?

You: _____

Me: _____

Do you agree that you must learn to respectfully agree to disagree with your spouse on some things, because not everything is going to be resolved or agreed on in your marriage?

You: Yes   No

Me: Yes   No

Do you agree to try to take a break when you notice yourself or your spouse starting to get too emotionally charged?

You: Yes   No

Me: Yes   No

What are some ways you can segue into a cooling down period when tensions build, without making matters worse?

_____

_____

_____

_____

_____

_____

_____

How can you implement clarifying into your daily life and disagreements with your spouse?

You: _____

_____

_____

_____

_____

Me: _____

_____

_____

_____

_____

Activity: Pick a topic you and your spouse need to resolve, and implement the 7 steps listed on page 114 as you communicate through it.

Learn to Apologize

Read Learn to Apologize, pages 115-116

What is hard for you when it comes to apologizing to your spouse?

You: _____

_____

_____

_____

_____

Me: _____

_____

_____

_____

_____

How do you give an apology to your spouse?

You: _____

_____

_____

_____

_____

Me: _____

_____

_____

_____

_____

How do you receive apologies best?

You: _____

_____

_____

_____

_____

Me: _____

_____

_____

_____

_____

Why are apologies important to you, or unimportant?

You: _____

_____

_____

_____

_____

Me: _____

_____

_____

_____

_____

What can you each do to make apologizing a part of your marriage, if it isn't already?

You: _____

_____

_____

_____

_____

Me: _____

_____

_____

_____

_____

How do you feel about apologizing to your spouse that their feelings were hurt,
even if that was never your intention?

You: _____

_____

_____

_____

_____

Me: _____

_____

_____

_____

_____

Activity: Is there anything that you feel you should apologize to your spouse for now? Then do it!

"I'm really sorry for _____. I know that made you feel _____, and I promise to do my best to not let it happen again. I love you, and I do not want to hurt you."

Don't Keep Score

Read Don't Keep Score, pages 117-119

Do you feel like you and your spouse are on the same team? Explain your answer.

You: _____

_____

_____

_____

_____

Me: _____

_____

_____

_____

_____

Do you feel like your spouse keeps score? Explain your answer.

You: _____

_____

_____

_____

_____

Me: _____

_____

_____

_____

_____

Do you feel like there is a power struggle in your marriage? Explain your answer.

You: _____

_____

_____

_____

_____

Me: _____

_____

_____

_____

_____

Do you feel that you have to be right when you have disagreements?

You:	Yes	No
Me:	Yes	No

Do you agree that almost everything can have more than one way to get it done, or have more than one solution to a problem?

You:	Yes	No
Me:	Yes	No

Do you ever feel like your spouse brings up old things to hold over your head?
Explain your answer.

You: _____

_____

_____

_____

_____

Me: _____

_____

_____

_____

Can you both agree to not keep score, guilt, or
bring up old hurts/mistakes from here on out?

You: Yes   No

Me: Yes   No

Do you ever feel like your spouse tries to guilt you into doing things or going places?
Explain your answer.

You: _____

_____

_____

_____

_____

Me: _____

_____

_____

_____

Do you ever feel like you need your spouse's permission? What for?

You: _____

_____

_____

_____

Me: _____

_____

_____

_____

Chapter 7

Read 7 Steps for Getting Started, pages 121-126

What has prevented you from learning the skills needed to become a better communicator with your spouse?

You: _____

_____

_____

_____

_____

Me: _____

_____

_____

_____

_____

These seven steps summarize how you can better communicate with your spouse. Write down how you will implement each one; remind yourself, and your spouse, to keep these steps in mind; and put them into action.

Step 1. May I have your attention, please?

You: _____

_____

_____

_____

_____

Me: _____

_____

_____

_____

_____

Step 2. No yelling.

You: _____

_____

_____

_____

_____

Me: _____

_____

_____

_____

_____

Step 3. A mile in your spouse's shoes.

You: _____

_____

_____

_____

_____

Me: _____

_____

_____

_____

_____

Step 4. Confirm understanding.

You: _____

_____

_____

_____

_____

Me: _____

_____

_____

_____

Step 5. Change your style.

You: _____

_____

_____

_____

Me: _____

_____

_____

_____

Step 6. Take a break.

You: _____

_____

_____

_____

Me: _____

_____

_____

_____

_____

Step 7. Rinse and repeat.

You: _____

_____

_____

_____

_____

Me: _____

_____

_____

_____

_____

Your 7-Day Action Plan

For the next seven days, start implementing the 7 steps, one at a time, through your daily interactions with your spouse. Start with one or two things at a time, like working on your tone while speaking to your spouse and listening empathetically. Then add on as you feel comfortable. You can practice these skills with other family members and close friends for extra practice too.

Visit www.ourpeacefulfamily.com/7dayworksheet to get your copy of the 7-Day Worksheet we created to make it easier for you to practice.

Now, go back to the goals you set at the beginning of this workbook and reflect on them after the seventh day.

- » Have you achieved these goals?

- » Do you have the tools to achieve those goals?

What did you learn in this book that really stuck out to you?

You: _____

_____

_____

_____

Me: _____

_____

_____

_____

Thank You

Congratulations on completing this workbook. We are very thankful and excited to help you learn how to communicate with your spouse and build a strong foundation for your marriage.

If you enjoyed this book, please leave us a review and rating on Amazon.

We would love to know how this communication workbook impacts you and your marriage, and what we can do to make it better. Also, if you found this workbook useful, please share it with other couples who might as well.

You can also send us an email with any questions you have about communication in marriage to: firstyearmarriage@gmail.com.

We cannot promise that we will immediately reply to every email, due to the volume of emails we receive, but we will do our best to cover your question in future blog posts or podcast episodes.

If you would like to receive email updates about future books, bonuses, plus get your FREE 7-Day Worksheet, visit the website below:

www.ourpeacefulfamily.com/7dayworksheet

Thank you again for choosing and completing our communication workbook!

Marcus and Ashley Kusi

Enjoy your marriage, enjoy your life!

About Marcus and Ashley

We help overwhelmed newlyweds adjust to married life, and inspire married couples to improve their marriage so they can become better husbands and wives.

We do this by using our own marriage experience, gleaning wisdom from other seasoned couples, and sharing what works for us through our website and marriage podcast, *The First Year Marriage Show*.

Visit the website below to listen to the podcast:

www.firstyearmarriage.com

Visit our website to learn more about us:

www.ourpeacefulfamily.com

Marriage is a life-long journey that thrives on love, commitment, trust, respect, communication, patience, and companionship.

– Ashley and Marcus Kusi

Other Books by Marcus and Ashley

1) **Communication in Marriage**: How to Communicate with Your Spouse Without Fighting

2) **Questions for Couples**: 469 Thought-Provoking Conversation Starters for Connecting, Building Trust, and Rekindling Intimacy

3) **Our Bucket List Adventures:** A Journal for Couples

4) **First Year of Marriage**: The Newlywed's Guide to Building a Strong Foundation and Adjusting to Married Life.

5) **Emotional and Sexual Intimacy in Marriage**: How to Connect or Reconnect with Your Spouse, Grow Together, and Strengthen Your Marriage

6) **Mama Bear Kusi's Blank Recipe Book**: A Journal with Templates to Write and Organize All Your Favorite Recipes.

7) **Mama Bear Kusi's Weekly Meal Planner**: A 52-Week Menu Planner with Grocery List for Planning Your Meals.

8) **My Tandem Nursing Journey**: Breastfeeding Through Pregnancy, Labor, Nursing Aversion and Beyond.

Made in the
USA
Middletown, DE